SCOTLAND'S

Animal Superstars

True Stories About Braw Birds & Beasties

by

Kimberlie Hamilton

pokey hat

cranachan

For John,
who shared many adventures with
me while researching this book.

Unicorn

Loch Ness Monster

Wild Haggis

What's the most famous animal in Scotland?

Is it the Loch Ness Monster?

Greyfriars Bobby?

Or maybe it's the mythical unicorn, Scotland's national animal?

(It definitely isn't haggis, which isn't even an animal at all!)

Although these legendary creatures are awesome, there are real-life animals in Scotland that deserve to be celebrated, too-including World War Two heroes, military mascots, furry ambassadors, and social media stars!

Get to know 25 of them just by turning the page...

Contents

Bamse Wartime Hero

How is it that a family pet from Norway became a war hero in Scotland? That's exactly what happened to a lovable Saint Bernard named Bamse.

Bamse belonged to the Captain of a whaling ship called the *Thorodd*. When World War Two began, the ship was drafted into service—and so were the Captain and Bamse! When the Nazis invaded Norway, the *Thorodd* escaped to Scotland to continue the fight. Stationed in Dundee and Montrose, it was used to find and remove explosive naval mines.

All the sailors adored Bamse. In the midst of battle, the pony-sized hound stood at the bow of the ship in his steel helmet, inspiring everyone to fight on. Whenever the ship was docked, he headed ashore to have a wee wander. He gave children rides on his back, broke up pub brawls and escorted sailors back to the ship before curfew. He even had his very own bus pass!

When the Captain was posted to another ship, the crew of the *Thorodd* refused to let him take Bamse with him.

Their furry mascot was so important for morale that the Captain agreed to leave him in their care until the war was over.

Bamse's reputation spread after he saved the lives of two men. One time, a robber attacked an officer with a knife but Bamse knocked him into the harbour. Another time, he rescued a sailor from drowning after the man fell overboard, unseen by anyone else.

Bamse held a special place in the hearts of Scots and Norwegians alike. When his big heart gave out at last, he was buried in Montrose with full military honours.

Several hundred of his friends, many of them children, came to his funeral. People still visit his gravesite today, often leaving a stone behind to show they were there.

BAMSE'S LEGACY

In 2006, Prince Andrew unveiled a larger-than-life-sized bronze statue of Sea Dog Bamse on the waterfront in Montrose, facing towards Norway. There's an identical statue in Bamse's Norwegian hometown, Honningsvåg, facing towards Scotland.

THE PDSA GOLD MEDAL

Many years after his death, Bamse was honoured for his bravery and devotion to duty with the PDSA Gold Medal. He is the only WW2 animal to ever earn this prestigious award.

Artist's Inspiration

Baron was something of a local celebrity in Glasgow, where the Clydesdale horse lived for many years at Pollok Country Park. But he gained even greater fame when he served as a model for the massive horse sculptures The Kelpies.

As large as he was, Baron was kind and gentle, happy to be stroked and fussed over by his adoring fans. Baron was such a gentleman, he was even a guest of honour at the wedding of his long-time handler, Lorraine. They had a very close bond, especially after a scary experience they once had together.

Lorraine was out for a ride on her four-legged friend when they came to a foot bridge over a burn. Baron stopped dead in his tracks and refused to cross it. Lorraine had made the same crossing on another horse and couldn't understand why Baron felt uneasy. She insisted that he walk on.

As he stepped out onto the bridge, the whole thing collapsed! They dropped into the water and Baron scrambled back up the bank. Lorraine never doubted his horse sense again.

Lorraine & Baron

4

Baron gained worldwide fame thanks to *The Kelpies*, two huge steel sculptures located in Falkirk. The artist wanted two Clydesdales to serve as his models for the project. Baron was the model for the heads-up kelpie and his work buddy, Duke, for the heads-down kelpie. Without them, designing the sculptures would have been much more difficult.

THE KELPIES are 30-metre high horse heads that took three months to build. Each one weighs 300 tons and is made up of 928 stainless steel plates. They are the largest equine statues in the world!

When Baron visited the sculptor at his studio, he came clattering out of his trailer and towered over everyone, tossing his head in the bright sunshine. Yet he stood so still and calm as the artist examined him and took countless photos, it seemed like he understood what a big deal *The Kelpies* project was.

Baron passed away in 2017 but his likeness will stand for generations to come, a proud and majestic symbol of Scotland.

IN CELTIC FOLKLORE kelpies are shape-shifting water spirits that often took the form of horses.

Cruachan IV Pony Mascot

Corporal Cruachan IV is well known for many things, but perhaps most of all for his close encounters with the Royal Family.

The Royal Regiment of Scotland mascot once tried to nibble Her Majesty the Queen's posy during a visit to Stirling Castle. Another time, he let out a loud whinny to welcome the monarch to Balmoral Castle, prompting her to say, "We know where you are!"

Balmoral Castle

The tradition of having a Shetland pony mascot dates way back to 1929. That's when Queen Victoria's daughter, Princess Louise, presented a black pony to the Argyll and Sutherland Highlanders. The soldiers named him Cruachan, the battle cry of the Campbell clan.

Since then only three other Shetlands have held the position, and all of them have been black with a white star on their forehead.

The Queen had to give her approval before Cruachan could begin his training. He now sees Her Majesty quite often, especially at Balmoral, where he spends part of each summer during her annual visit. Sometimes she visits him and slips him a few Polo mints, his favourite sweet treat!

Cruachan also made headlines for taking a cheeky swipe at Prince Harry's fingers, which made the Duchess of Sussex giggle.

Cruachan keeps a busy schedule, officially representing Scotland at parades, fairs, Highland Games and other special events. He is a soldier and is expected to act like a soldier, and he is well aware when he's getting his photo taken. He proudly acts like he's three feet taller whenever he wears his formal military uniform.

THE EDINBURGH TATTOO

The Edinburgh Military Tattoo is one of the biggest events of the year for Cruachan IV and the Royal Regiment. It's held each August at Edinburgh Castle, with hundreds of Scottish soldiers in kilts performing music and marching in formation. Cruachan's handler, the Regiment's Pony Major, used to pack cotton wool in his ears to soften the noise. All those bagpipes and drums and fireworks are LOUD.

Dolly

Famous Cloned Sheep

Dolly the Sheep was unlike any other animal born in Scotland in 1996. She started off life in a petri dish!

Dolly was cloned from cells from a Finn Dorset sheep and a Scottish Blackface sheep. Then a surrogate mother—another Scottish Blackface—carried and gave birth to her at a laboratory in Edinburgh.

The newborn lamb was the world's first animal cloned from an adult cell, something no one at the time thought was possible. Dolly was a genetic carbon copy of her mum's DNA.

Dolly's history-making birth was kept super-duper top secret for quite some time. When the big news was finally announced, people around the world were pretty gobsmacked, to say the least.

News reporters and photographers couldn't get enough of Dolly and her story, but she wasn't fazed by all the lights and noise and camera crews. She was like a farm animal rock star—not bad for a sheep!

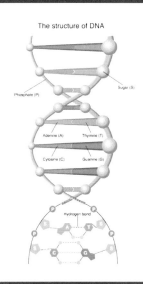

The structure of DNA

Phosphate (P)

Sugar (S)

Adenine (A)   Thymine (T)

Cytosine (C)   Guanine (G)

Hydrogen bond

Of course, not everyone was thrilled by this scientific breakthrough. There were all sorts of arguments over whether or not cloning animals was a good idea. Where would it all lead? Would people be cloned one day? What might this do to the human race? The debate goes on to this day.

MAD BUT TRUE
Dolly was named after the famous American country singer Dolly Parton.

Once all the fuss was over, Dolly went on to lead a perfectly ordinary life with a flock of perfectly ordinary sheep.

She had six lambs with a ram named David, including a set of twins and a set of triplets. Her adorable babies all came into the world the good old-fashioned way—in a pasture, not a lab. Baaaaa!

After her death, Dolly's body was preserved and donated to the National Museum of Scotland in Edinburgh.

You can still go and see her there inside a big glass case, where she is one of the museum's most popular exhibits.

SCOTTISH FOLDS

Dolly was created by scientists. But sometimes a new kind of animal is created by chance, something called a natural genetic mutation. That's exactly what happened with the Scottish Fold cat. Every member of the breed can be traced back to Susie, a cat with folded, owl-like ears that was born in Scotland in the 1960s.

Donald Death-Defying Duck

In the dark days of the Second World War, far from home in the Far East, a Scottish soldier saved a baby duck as it was being swept down a river after a storm. This life-or-death moment would change both their futures forever.

Corporal William Gray named the orphan duckling after a well-known cartoon character. Donald seemed a fine Scottish name for the new 'mascot' of the Gordon Highlanders. They were a Scottish regiment whose 2nd Battalion was being held as prisoners of war (POWs).

Except for one thing—Donald was a girl! That became quite clear the day she proudly presented Willie with her first egg. The name stuck nevertheless.

2876971 Gray, William

The prison guards wanted to make a tasty meal out of Donald but Willie was much too clever for them. He said Donald was a sacred bird that he and his fellow Scotsmen had to fall down and worship each morning. It was a crazy thing to say, but it actually worked.

The POWs suffered terribly, forced to work hard for 18 hours a day with nothing more than some plain rice to eat. Donald's eggs provided much-needed protein that helped keep the half-starved soldiers alive.

When the war ended, the men of the Regiment couldn't wait to get back home. They were ordered to leave everything behind, including pets. Willie refused to abandon Donald and smuggled her aboard the troop transport ship. She was soon discovered and he pleaded for her life to be spared. Once again, his words worked their magic and his little feathered friend was allowed to stay.

Back on British soil, Willie and his duck headed north to Aberdeen. A newspaper photographer snapped their picture as Willie stepped off the train with Donald in his arms.

Onlookers watched with delight as Donald waddled down the street after her beloved master. Then she was treated to a glass of beer at a nearby pub! The unlikely pair went on to live happily ever after together in the Scottish countryside.

LIKE A DUCK TO WATER

Willie and a neighbour help Donald introduce her ducklings to water for the first time.

MAD BUT TRUE

On the long and chilly voyage back to Scotland, some kind-hearted Gordon Highlanders knitted a teeny tiny jumper to keep Donald warm!

Golden George
Scotland's Ambassadog

When VisitScotland launched a nationwide search for a canine ambassador, they were looking for a very special dog. One that could serve as a four-legged representative of the spirit of Scotland.

Over 200 dogs applied and eight furry contenders made it to the finals. It was a tough competition but in the end there could only be one Ambassadog. Golden George, a Golden retriever from Glasgow, nabbed the coveted role.

George's main duties are to get out and meet people and promote Scotland and its natural beauty. He has the perfect personality for this, curious and full of energy, eager to explore and make new friends wherever he goes.

And George has a LOT of friends, including more than 18,000 followers on Instagram.

Since being named Ambassadog in 2016, George has been all over Scotland.

He's splashed about in Loch Lomond. He wore a special camera to film scenes in Fife from a dog's point of view. He rode a ferry all the way to the Outer Hebrides.

He's even been a VID (Very Important Dog) at a posh hotel in Edinburgh, where he slept in a fancy dog bed and posed for selfies with fans.

One of George's favourite experiences was strutting down the red carpet at the *Isle of Dogs* premiere at the Glasgow Film Festival.

Another highlight was visiting the Royal Yacht Britannia, which once belonged to Her Majesty the Queen. Dogs usually aren't allowed on board but the crew made a rare exception for George. He is, after all, Scotland's Ambassadog!

GOLDEN OPPORTUNITY

Many people don't know that Golden retrievers were first bred in Scotland. Not long ago, there was a huge gathering at Lord Tweedmouth's ancestral home to celebrate the 150th anniversary of the breed. More than 360 Goldens showed up for the party!

TOO CUTE!

FRIENDS FUREVER

Golden George gets along great with other animals. He was invited once to a corgi "meet-up", where he towered over his short-legged pals, and one of his best mates is a cat named Gus.

GREYFRIARS BOBBY

George is pretty famous but Greyfriars Bobby is the stuff of legend. As the story goes, Bobby refused to leave his master's grave for 14 years.

Legions of tourists come to Edinburgh to visit the statue of the faithful Skye terrier. So many have rubbed his nose for luck that it's nearly worn away!

Hamish ★ The ★ Highland Bull

Hamish was very likely the most photographed Highland bull of all time. He rose to fame after his life nearly ended when he was just a youngster.

He started his working life at an art museum in Stirling, of all places. The museum was hosting an exhibition of works by a Victorian painter who specialized in animal art, using real animals as his models.

The curator drew attention to the show by bringing in a small herd of farm animals to wander about the museum's grounds. Hamish was one, and the sight of him literally stopped traffic.

But then something terrible happened. There was an illness going around Britain in 1996 known as Mad Cow Disease. Some said that every cow and bull aged three and up should be put down to keep the disease from spreading. Including poor Hamish! Animal lovers kicked up such a fuss with a *Save Hamish* campaign that his life was spared.

The campaign made Hamish a national celebrity. He appeared on TV, pulled Santa's sleigh and visited a pub—and a china shop, too! He posed for thousands of selfies, had his own Facebook page and received cards and gifts for his birthday and Christmas.

After he retired to a woollen mill in Perthshire, so many overseas visitors came to see him that an information sign was posted in four languages.

Hamish was the only one of his kind at the mill for quite some time. Then he was introduced to a young cow named Heather. The first time he saw her he was so excited that he did a little "Highland fling" to impress her. Hamish and Heather were very happy together and had a baby named Honey. And every Valentine's Day, Hamish gave his beloved a single red rose. Awww!

Hamish lived to the ripe old age of 23, which made him the world's second oldest Highland bull. He remains one of Scotland's greatest (and hairiest) legends.

A MUCKLE COO...
is a great big beastie, and Hamish was certainly that.

He was built to withstand Scotland's winters, with an extra-long coat that kept body heat in and cold weather out.

His large feet were made for walking over boggy ground. His long fringe kept wind, rain, sun and bugs out of his eyes. He also had a grand pair of long, curved horns.

SAY WHAT?
In Scotland, Highland Cow is pronounced "heelan coo". Just in case you're wondering what people are talking about!

FUN FACT! Hamish's favourite treat was a handful of fresh strawberries.

Grizzly goes to Hollywood

Hercules was one of the biggest stars in Scotland once upon a time, in more ways than one.

He lived with a former pro wrestler and his wife, who bought him from a wildlife park as a wee cub. Hercules became a member of their family, and he grew to be more than 2.5 metres tall and weighed a whopping 500kg! Grizzly bears may be among the world's most dangerous mammals, but Hercules was a big softie. In fact, Big Softie was one of his nicknames!

Hercules made a name for himself as a wrestling bear but gained even greater fame when he went missing in 1980. He ran off while filming an advert in the Outer Hebrides and was lost for 24 days. Everyone had just about given up hope when a crofter finally spotted him.

Poor Hercules! In the hours after his return, the half-starved bear guzzled down 120 pints of milk and dozens and dozens of eggs. He had lost more than half his body weight, as he'd opted to go hungry rather than harm another living creature for food. This endeared Hercules all the more to people, even those who had feared him most.

Hercules went on to play a role in a James Bond film starring Roger Moore. He moved to Hollywood for a while and had his photo on the cover of *Time* magazine. He played golf with a famous American comedian and was named "Personality of the Year" by the Scottish Tourist Board. He even received letters from U.S. President Ronald Reagan and Her Majesty the Queen.

FEEDING HERCULES

It took a LOT of food to feed a big bear like Hercules. He started his day with a loaf of bread, baked beans, four fried eggs and sweet coffee. For a morning snack he had fruit and yoghurt, then another loaf of bread topped with beans for lunch. After a snack in the afternoon, he tucked into a hearty supper, like fish and chips washed down with a bottle of Irn-Bru.

Hercules (1974 - 2001)

Despite his success, Hercules never let fame go to his gigantic grizzly head. He was always happiest when he was at home with his family in Scotland.

GONE BUT NOT FORGOTTEN

Hercules died when he was 25 and was buried on the island of North Uist in the Outer Hebrides. The site is marked by a life-sized statue of him.

Kylie

Bilingual Dolphin

Kylie has been the only dolphin in the Firth of Clyde on Scotland's west coast for a long time. But she might not be as lonely as people once thought—she's learned how to "speak" porpoise!

It's believed that Kylie somehow became separated from her pod many years ago. Yet marine biologists studying underwater recordings now suspect that she is making new friends in a most unusual way.

She has changed the clicking sounds she uses for navigating and hunting so the porpoises can understand her.

Why is this such a big deal? This may be the first time ever that a dolphin like Kylie has learned how to communicate with a different species. It's sort of like a cat learning how to talk to a dog! That definitely makes her one of Scotland's animal superstars.

CAN YOU TELL A DOLPHIN FROM A PORPOISE?

Dolphins are bigger and have pointed snouts, porpoises are smaller with rounded snouts. Both are marine mammals but it is VERY rare for dolphins and porpoises to hang out with each other. That's why Kylie's story is so amazing!

Kylie has been featured on the radio and on a BBC TV programme seen by millions of viewers. Her new-found fame has made her something of a tourist attraction, which isn't necessarily a good thing. All the noise from boats, jet skis, and construction work in the harbour are disturbing her rest and making her stressed out.

A new viewing platform is now in the works so that people can enjoy watching Kylie from a safe distance.

People concerned about Kylie's well-being were inspired to create a new flavour of ice cream in her honour. Kylie's Flipperberry Ripple is a colourful mixture of unicorn flavour (which is pink), glittery sherbet and blue bubblegum.

Everyone who buys an ice cream also gets a leaflet about how to keep the Firth of Clyde clean and quiet and safe so that no harm ever comes to Kylie and her porpoise friends.

Do not disturb

YUM!

KEEPING DOLPHINS SAFE

- Stay at least 100 metres away.

- Shhh! Leave them alone, especially during the day when dolphins like to rest.

- Never swim with, touch or feed a dolphin. Getting too familiar with humans can be dangerous for them.

Oswald MUSEUM MOGGY

Oswald is the Cat-in-Charge at the Stirling Smith Art Gallery and Museum. He has so many important duties that he actually lives there 24/7.

The black-and-white moggy was for many years the personal advisor to the museum's long-time director. Now that she's retired, his top job is protecting the Smith's collections. Oswald's nightly patrols have made him well acquainted with every work of art and historical artefact in the place.

His favourite exhibit is something very rare and precious—the world's oldest football!

Oswald keeps fit by chasing rabbits and mice off the Smith's two acres of grounds. He also does regular walkabouts to make sure the beautiful gardens are kept up to scratch.

He has the volunteer gardeners so well trained that they planted a nose-high patch of catnip just for him.

When he isn't taste-testing cakes in the café, attending lectures, or greeting visitors at the door, Oswald sees to his office duties. He's a deft paw with a computer mouse and has been known to send cryptic e-mails in the dead of night. He's also active on social media, offering a cat's-eye perspective on museum events.

Tweet Oswald: @Smithsupercat

There was a scary period not long ago when it looked like the Smith might be closed down.

Oswald worked hard to help keep the doors open, urging his fans to sign a petition to *Save the Smith*.

His photo even appeared on the front page of the local newspaper with the headline, *"It Would Be a Cat-astrophe to Shut Smith".* Luckily, it worked!

Oswald has devoted the past 15 years of his life to the Smith. Whatever needs to be done, he can be relied on to do his part, even if it means sprawling on the floor so visitors can admire and stroke his fur. Free of charge, of course, just like the museum itself.

CASTLE KITTY
Oswald's domain is just a stone's throw from Stirling Castle, the childhood home of Mary Queen of Scots. Her father, King James V, kept a big cat in the castle's courtyard, which was known as the Lion's Den.

Parsley Town Cat of Oban

Parsley lives in Oban, a pretty harbour town on Scotland's west coast. Although he's never set a paw beyond its borders, the big ginger cat has more than 8,000 Facebook friends around the world!

Parsley has been a wanderer ever since he was a kitten, popping into shops and hotels and strangers' homes just to say hello. He invites himself to parties and visits beauty salons, fish and chip shops, and artist studios.

One Sunday he went to services at two different churches. Another time, he was spotted lounging on a piano at a music store. He even strolled aboard a ship docked in the harbour. Who knows where he might have ended up if he hadn't been found in time!

GPS Tracker

MIAOW

His human mum gave up trying to guess Parsley's whereabouts and put a GPS tracker on his collar. She was astonished to learn that her curious kitty walked about three to four miles a day.

Parsley's personal best was six miles in 24 hours! He wandered so far that the police grew concerned and escorted him home in their van. Sooooo embarrassing.

After making the rounds of all the pubs in Oban, Parsley finally decided that The Balmoral was his favourite. He sits by the door or sprawls on the bar for hours at a time. A taxi had to be sent there once when his mum couldn't go fetch him herself.

Maine Coons are known for being super friendly and hanging out at tourist hotspots has allowed him to meet all kinds of people. Some travel miles and miles to see him after following his adventures (and misadventures) on Facebook. Yet as busy as he is, Parsley still finds time to volunteer for Hope Kitchen, where he hosts a weekly One Cat Café. After all, when you have a one-of-a-kind feline like Parsley, one cat is really all you need!

PURRFECTLY IMPERFECT

Parsley is mellow moggy but prefers not to be stroked too much. He never purrs, rarely meows and has zero interest in mice. His quirkiness is a big part of his feline charm. As Parsley sees it, you don't have to be perfect to be purrrfect!

THE MINISTER OF CATS

Parsley has such a keen interest in politics that he's appointed himself the Minister of Cats for Scotland.

HAMISH MCHAMISH

Scotland had another famous town cat, Hamish McHamish, a ginger moggy that lived in the university town of St. Andrews. After he passed away at age 15, the town put up a life-sized statue of him.

PD SWEEP Super Sniffer Dog

Police Dog Sweep was a Cocker Spaniel that worked as a detection dog. He helped the police find all kinds of stuff, like illegal drugs, weapons, and cash. He was the UK's only poison detection dog too!

When PD Sweep was just a tiny pup, he loved to run about, slide across slippery floors and race up the stairs. But his favourite thing of all was to explore new places, sticking his nose into everything. That was a very good sign that he might make a great sniffer dog.

PD Sweep's police training started right away. First, he had to form a close bond with his handler, a police constable named Rhona. Then he learned how to respond to her whistled commands and search for balls that she had carefully hidden from him.

Next up was a special course on finding drugs, followed by training on finding guns and ammunition. PD Sweep learned how to locate bundles of cash that belonged to bad guys, too.

When PD Sweep caught the scent of whatever the police were searching for, he would sit or lie down to signal that he'd found something. A day on the job for PD Sweep was sort of like being on a super important scavenger hunt. He used his fab sense of smell to sniff out clues that humans couldn't detect.

PD Sweep hard at work sniffing suitcases at the airport!

PD Sweep's biggest find was in a flat that had already been searched high and low. The police were stumped—they knew drugs were in there somewhere but couldn't find them. So they called in their furry expert to do what he does best. Within a matter of minutes, he found the stash. And can you guess where it was? Hidden inside a sofa!

SIR SWEEP

In his eight years on duty, PD Sweep tracked down drugs and cash worth hundreds of thousands of pounds, as well as a heap of dangerous guns and ammunition.

He was awarded the PDSA Order of Merit for all his hard work fighting against crime in Scotland. This very impressive honour is considered the OBE for animals!

PD Sweep on his day off!

Peggy prisoner of war

All sorts of animals have been adopted by Scottish soldiers over the years, including dogs, cats, goats and monkeys. One was Peggy, a white bull terrier. She was the official mascot of the Gordon Highlanders 2nd Battalion, a regiment of the British Army based in Singapore during World War Two.

The war in the Pacific began in 1941, when Japan attacked Singapore and Hawaii. The Gordon Highlanders were ordered to fight—and Peggy went into combat with them. When the soldiers became prisoners of war (POWs), Peggy stayed with them and lived on rice and scraps, just as they did. When the POWs were forced to do hard labour, Peggy marched with them to and from their place of work each day.

The POWs in the Far East were treated very badly. Thousands died, including almost 400 of the Gordon Highlanders. Peggy did her best to protect her friends from harm, alerting them of approaching danger and growling at the guards who beat them. This made the guards so angry that they beat her too, but Peggy was tough enough to survive her injuries.

After three and a half miserable years in prison camps, the war finally ended. The men of the 2nd Battalion were to be flown to Burma, the first stage of their journey back to Scotland.

But what about Peggy? No animals were allowed aboard troop transport planes or ships, but a case was made that Peggy was an official Army mascot that didn't deserve to be left behind. Eventually, the rules were waived and Peggy was allowed to travel to her new home in a land far, far away.

Peggy spent some time in quarantine before rejoining her soldier friends in Aberdeen, where she was hailed as a canine war hero and awarded the same four medals as her fellow POWs.

RIP PEGGY

When Peggy died in 1947, her longtime champion—Lieutenant Colonel Reggie Lees—had a granite gravestone made to honour her memory. It can be seen today outside the Gordon Highlanders Museum in Aberdeen.

Sheila

Sheila's story is the tale of a dramatic wartime rescue that sounds like something out of a Hollywood film.

As a working dog on a farm, Sheila wasn't allowed to enter military service as many other canines did during the Second World War. And so it was that in December 1944, she was at her home in Scotland's Borders region when a plane crashed in the nearby Cheviot Hills.

It was a B17 Flying Fortress, a U.S. bomber carrying a crew of six. Two of the men lost their lives on impact. Four others survived, only to find themselves lost in a blizzard, miles and miles from anywhere.

John Dagg
& Sheila

Three local shepherds raced to the crash site, including John Dagg and his faithful sheepdog Sheila. The wind was ferocious and they could hardly see in the whiteout conditions.

Upon reaching the top of the hill, Sheila disappeared into the whirling snow. She swiftly found the air crew, huddled together for warmth in a nearby ravine.

Sheila raced back to her master and calmly and confidently guided him to the half-frozen men.

The ordeal wasn't over yet. The wreckage of the plane was on fire and the Americans warned their rescuers to stay far away from it. There was a real risk that the bombs on board might blow.

And sure enough, as soon as the shepherds and crew reached the safety of Mr Dagg's croft, the plane's bombs exploded with enough force to shatter windows. BOOM!

BOOM!!

For her skill and bravery, Sheila was made an honorary member of British Forces Mascot Club. She was also awarded a PDSA Dickin Medal, the highest honour any wartime animal can receive. Sheila is still to this day the only non-military dog to ever earn it.

FROM ONE MUM TO ANOTHER

Sheila's only puppy, Tibbie, was later flown to America to live with the mother of one of the crew members killed in the crash.

WAR DOGS MEMORIAL

Other canine war heroes from Scotland are honoured with a new memorial featuring life-size Airedale terriers and their handlers. The statue is located at Easthaven (near Carnoustie), where the dogs were trained during World War Two. These dedicated and hard-working hounds served as guard dogs, delivered messages, moved supplies, carried ammunition and brought first aid to wounded soldiers.

Sir Nils Olav
Penguin Brigadier

Edinburgh Zoo has long been famous for its colony of penguins. And the most famous of these penguins is an upstanding fellow by the name of Sir Nils Olav. Believe it or not, he is a brigadier in the Royal Norwegian Guard.

The story of how this came about began way back in 1913, when Norway presented the zoo with three King penguins.

They were the first penguins ever seen outside the South Atlantic!

Many years later, a lieutenant in the Royal Guard visited the zoo and found himself fascinated by the penguins.

He arranged for his unit to adopt one of the flightless birds as their mascot, naming it after himself (naturally) and the then-king of Norway, Olav V.

As the Royal Guards' newest member, Nils Olav rose rapidly through the ranks, promoted each time his regiment came to visit him in Scotland.

So far there have been three penguins named Nils Olav. After the first one died, he was replaced by Nils Olav II, who became the first penguin to receive a knighthood. He was knighted at a lavish ceremony attended by 130 guardsmen and hundreds of spectators.

Standing proud and ramrod straight, Sir Nils was on his best behaviour as a declaration from the Norwegian king was read aloud. The honour was bestowed in the traditional way, with the gentle tap of a sword.

A third penguin, Sir Nils Olav III, was next in line.

He was promoted to Brigadier and now wears his fancy military insignia on his right flipper whenever there is a special occasion.

Brigadier is the highest rank in the Norwegian Army, so any lower ranking soldiers are required to formally salute him. Yes, really!

PENGUINS ON PARADE

Penguins strut around the grounds of the Edinburgh Zoo every afternoon, something they've done since the 1950s. The tradition started when a zookeeper accidentally left a gate open and was followed around the zoo by a conga line of penguins.
Visitors were so delighted that it became a regular thing.

Smudge Palace Cat

Smudge was a famous mouser at the People's Palace, a museum in Scotland's largest city. Her proper title was Chief Rodent Control Officer and she took great pride in her work.

Other museum workers belonged to a trade union, which was sort of like a club for City of Glasgow employees. Smudge wanted to join too but her application was turned down. And for no good reason except that she was a CAT. So unfair!

Smudge's whiskers were in a bit of twist over this snub. Luckily, another trade union said she was purrfectly welcome to join their ranks.

She did, becoming the only cat to ever belong to a trade union, with her own membership card and everything. She later became the first cat in history to prowl the picket line during a workers' strike.

As the years went by, Smudge went from museum mouser to minor celebrity. She was a VIP guest at a big cat show and featured on the cover of book. She starred in ad campaigns for good causes, including one to save Glasgow's veterinary school.

There were even ceramic "replicats" made in her likeness, created by a renowned artist and sold to raise funds for new office equipment.

Despite her growing fame, there were some who grumbled about having a cat on staff, even one as loyal and hard-working as Smudge.

The museum's cat-loving curator adopted Smudge and gave her a fine home to spend the rest of her years.

Now and then, Smudge would lend her talents to another museum to get their mice under control.

Sister Smudge
(c 1970 - 2000)
was a much loved employee
of the People's Palace
and the only cat ever to be a full
member of the GMB Union

Smudge lived a long time—nearly 30 years—and the Glasgow newspaper published her obituary when she died.

A stone memorial was placed outside the People's Palace Winter Gardens so her memory will endure forever.

ABOUT THAT NAME...

Smudge's oddball name was bestowed by the gardeners at the Winter Gardens. She was sometimes called Sister Smudge, just so everyone knew she was a girl!

KITTY OF CULTURE

When Glasgow was named the European City of Culture in 1990, Smudge's fans dubbed her the "Kitty of Culture". They gave her a fancy tag with Glasgow's coat of arms, which she proudly wore on her collar.

Socks

Moonwalking Shetland Pony

Shetlands are little ponies with BIG personalities. And this miniature Shetland just might have the biggest personality of all!

Socks loves to roll on the ground, get muddy and caper with his friends. He's a real character and enjoys nothing more than being the centre of attention. His sassy spirit attracted the interest of an award-winning director who came all the way to the Shetland Islands to meet him. He was looking for a pony to be in a new TV advert and chose Socks to be the star.

Socks had just two weeks to learn how to do a special dance move called the 'Moonwalk'. Luckily, he has natural talent and quickly mastered pawing at the ground and gliding backwards in a perfectly straight line.

The director also wanted Socks to have a wild and bushy, Rod Stewart-esque mane. So each day of the five day shoot, a hair stylist put in 40 hair extensions to give Socks a look fit for a Scottish rock star. Many hours were spent bleaching the extensions until they were as close to Socks' natural colour as possible. Between takes, the stylist fluffed up Socks's mane with a hair dryer!

The 60-second advert had Socks showing off his fancy footwork to impress the other ponies, nearly tumbling off a steep cliff and hiding his dance moves from a passing farmer. The slogan was, 'Silly stuff. It matters."

The video had more than 6 million hits on YouTube, making Socks an overnight sensation. He was featured on TV and interviewed for magazines and newspapers. A plush toy was made in his likeness and he even got a red nose for Comic Relief Day.

People still make the long journey up to the islands just to get a selfie with the famous moonwalking pony!

SMILE, YOU'RE ON CAMERA!

Socks's grin in the video is actually the expression he makes whenever he smells something he likes. Special effects artists enhanced his "smile" by making it even wider and brighter.

DID YOU KNOW?

Shetland ponies measure between 70 and 107 centimetres high at the withers (the ridge between their shoulder blades).

A Shetland pony is a long-term pet—they can live to be 30 years old!

Socks with his Stylist!

Susan Royal Sidekick

Susan was a Pembroke Corgi that held a special place in the heart of Her Majesty the Queen.

Her Majesty has loved dogs all her life, ever since her family had a corgi named Dookie when she was a young girl. But Susan was the first corgi that belonged to the Queen.

The puppy was a gift from her beloved father on her 18th birthday. From that day on, the Queen and her furry sidekick were always together. And when she married Prince Philip, Susan even went along on their honeymoon.

When Princess Elizabeth (as she was once known) became Queen Elizabeth, everyone had to curtsy to her—even her own sister and mother. The only one who didn't treat her any differently once she had a crown on her head was Susan. From the royal pooch's point of view, the monarch was simply the human she adored most in the world.

Life as a royal pet was certainly a cushy one. Susan was allowed to go pretty much wherever she wished in any of the Queen's many homes.

No one was allowed to touch or feed Susan except for the Queen. The royal chef prepared all her meals so she never once ate anything from a tin.

At night, she slept in a raised wicker basket lined with comfy cushions. She was invited to all the Queen's private parties and travelled with her on trips abroad.

If the Queen ever had to be away, she left detailed maps of where her staff was to take Susan for walks each day.

Despite her sweet foxy face and life of leisure, Susan could be a tad challenging at times. Some called her 'spirited' or 'feisty', but to others she was just plain naughty.

She also had a reputation for biting; Susan's victims included a police constable and the Royal Clockwinder. Ouch!

Susan went on to become the matriarch of a long, long, LONG line of corgis. More than 30 corgis owned by Her Majesty over the years could all be traced back to Susan.

FAITHFUL FRIEND

When Susan died, she was buried in the pet cemetery at Sandringham House.

The Queen wrote the inscription herself and made a sketch of how she wanted the gravestone to look.

FUN FACT!

Queen Victoria— Her Majesty's great-great granny—started the royal tradition of keeping dogs as pets.

She had more than 100 in her lifetime.

Talavera Drum Horse

Talavera was a drum horse for the Royal Scots Dragoon Guards, Scotland's oldest military regiment. Drum horses are typically the tallest, best looking and most powerful horses in the regiment, and she was certainly all that.

Drum horses have been a part of military life for centuries. Commanders used to relay orders across the battlefield via trumpeters and drummers, which was super loud and often scared off the enemy.

While the days of soldiers charging into battle on horseback are long gone, replaced by "mechanical horses" like tanks and armoured trucks, the drum horse tradition proudly lives on.

Her Majesty the Queen presented Talavera to the Dragoon Guards in 2002. She became their official mascot and made appearances at formal ceremonies and parades, where she definitely stood out in a crowd. Not only was she big and strong, she was able to stay calm despite crowd noise, traffic, and the vibrations of the drums.

One of the first things she had to learn was how to carry a very heavy load. More and more weight was slowly introduced until finally she was decked out in her full regalia—two big drums and a fancy bridle, breastplate and saddle. All that—plus a rider—could weigh as much as 130 kilograms!

Once, the Queen visited the Regiment's barracks and offered Talavera a treat. Talavera eagerly slurped it up, leaving a dollop of slobber on Her Majesty.

Luckily, the Queen is an expert with horses and took it in her stride, but it still made front page news the next day. Talavera likely wasn't too thrilled about that.

Talavera slevers on Queen!

After 14 years in the military, Talavera retired to The Horse Trust, a rest home for horses that have devoted their lives to public service.

But once a drum horse, always a drum horse—she's just as strong-willed as ever.

Talavera was named after a 17th century battle in Spain, but her nickname around the stable yard is much less formal—Pip!

THAT'S DRAGOON, NOT DRAGON!

The word dragoon once referred to soldiers who rode into battle on horseback in the 17th and 18th centuries.

Today, it refers to any ceremonial mounted regiment.

Torty Tortoise Time Capsule

As one of Scotland's oldest tower homes, Drum Castle has been around for more than seven centuries. And for 170 of those years, the family that lived there shared it with a rather unusual pet—a tortoise named Torty.

Despite being the castle's oldest resident, little is remembered about Torty. She's a bit of a mystery, which is a shame because she was something of a living time capsule.

She lived through two World Wars, 36 British Prime Ministers and nine British monarchs. She was born before Queen Victoria ascended the throne and lived years beyond the day astronauts walked on the moon. If only Torty could have talked! She'd have some stories to tell, that's for sure.

How did Torty come to live in Scotland? As the story goes, a friend of the Irvine family brought back two tortoises from some faraway land.

He presented one to Hampton Court Palace and gave the other to Drum Castle.

Back around the time of Torty's birth, world explorers were bringing back all sorts of never-before-seen animals to fill Britain's earliest zoos.

Some of these wild creatures were gifted to Queen Victoria, including lions, tigers, panthers, elephants, and an ostrich.

If you ever get a chance to visit Drum Castle, be sure to seek out Torty's humble gravestone in the family's pet cemetery.

For some reason her granite marker is inscribed **TORTY, 2.6.1988, AGED 149 YEARS.**

She was actually much older, but it's possible that her true age was deemed too mind boggling to believe. No one knows for sure, but it's fun to wonder about.

WHO KNEW?

Five young brothers lived in the castle in the early 1900s, the sons of the 22nd Laird of Drum.

They all thought Torty was a boy until 1927, when she surprised everyone by laying a few eggs.

Towser World Champ Mouser

Scotland is famous for its whisky and one of its oldest distilleries once had a famous distillery cat. Towser was such a brilliant mouser that she earned a spot in the Guinness Book of World Records!

Distilleries used to store lots of barley years ago, which was used to make whisky.

All that yummy grain attracted mice like bees to a honeypot, so many distilleries employed a feline rodent control expert like Towser.

Towser was born in 1963 and lived her entire life at Glenturret Distillery in Crieff. She was a beautiful tortoiseshell cat with long grey, silver and gold fur.

GUINNESS WORLD RECORDS

CERTIFICATE

The most prolific mouser is a female tortoiseshell cat named Towser, born on 21 April 1963 and owned by Glenturret Distillery Ltd near Crieff, Perth and Kinross, UK. Towser notched up an estimated 28,899 mice, averaging three mice per day until her death on 20 March 1987

OFFICIALLY AMAZING

Towser had such a talent for catching mice that she came to the attention of the Guinness Book of Records.

They sent out a team to watch her in action and concluded that she caught an average of three mice a day. Three mice a day every day of her long life added up to a head-spinning number—28,899 mice! That made her something of a feline 007, a skilled assassin with a license to kill.

The world's greatest mouser was still terrorising mice until she passed away shortly before her 24th birthday.

Towser's fame lives on at the distillery, where her life-sized bronze statue stands just outside the Visitor Centre.

Her paw prints also appear on the label of every bottle of a certain brand and there's even a special blend of whisky named in her honour. And rightly so!

TOWSER POWER

Towser may seem like a rather odd name for a cat but it's actually quite fitting.

One definition of "Towser" is "one full of energy," and that certainly describes her to a T. She needed a great deal of energy to keep all those pesky mice until control!

SCOTTISH WILDCATS

Towser looked a bit like a Scottish wildcat, an elusive species considered one of Scotland's last native predators.

Sadly, the "Highland Tiger" is nearly extinct—there are only about 35 wildcats left in the most remote parts of Scotland.

William Chapel Cat

Just south of Edinburgh is a 15th-century chapel made famous by a 20th-century book, 'The Da Vinci Code'. Yet Rosslyn Chapel is equally famous for its resident cat, a handsome tuxedo kitty called William.

William was named after the chapel's founder, Sir William St Clair, Prince of Orkney, whose Gothic masterpiece took 40 years to build.

Mysterious and symbolic stone carvings cover almost every surface inside and out, including exotic animals, plants, angels and unicorns.

Some have described the chapel as "a treasure in stone", and for very good reason.

In addition to chasing mice, it's William's job to keep a watchful eye on everything.

He attends church services and welcomes visitors, including the Canadian Prime Minister, who sat down with William for a proper chat.

He also enjoys weddings and once made himself comfy on the long train of a bride's dress, which made all the guests giggle.

William has become such a feline celebrity that people often come to Rosslyn Chapel just to see him.

His admirers can buy William souvenirs in the gift shop, such as a plush toy in his likeness. He is also featured in a charming picture book written by a real-life Countess.

Now how many cats can say that?

CAT NAP

If you ever visit the chapel, look for William snoozing in a pew or dozing atop a cosy heating vent.

When the weather is fine, he likes to stroll around the chapel's grounds, but he never strays too far. Rosslyn Chapel is his forever home and there's no place he would rather be.

MAISON DE MOGGY

Scotland's first cat café— Maison de Moggy—is located in nearby Edinburgh.

The cats at the café live there full-time and patrons can enjoy tea and cakes amongst purring pussycats. Awww!

Winkie Fearless Flyer

Winkie was the first pigeon credited with saving lives in World War Two, and for that she will never be forgotten.

On a cold winter day during World War Two, a Royal Air Force Beaufort bomber went down over the North Sea. The four men onboard had just enough time to send out a distress signal before plunging into the icy water.

They huddled in a life raft, knowing their chances of survival were slim. But they had one small hope—a pigeon with the code number NEHU.40.NS.1. In 1942, pigeons were often carried aboard planes as a back-up communication system.

Winkie the pigeon took to the air after being thrown free from her basket, and the men prayed she'd make it safely back to shore. She faced a long and difficult journey of 120 miles. It seemed like an impossible mission.

Against all odds, the pigeon managed to make it home by the next morning. Her owner found her, covered with oil and so exhausted that one eye wouldn't stop blinking.

He notified the RAF base and they matched her code number to the missing aircraft. They were also able to figure out the plane's position using the time difference between the last radio contact and the pigeon's arrival.

These coordinates were sent to a search party that was already out looking for the damaged bomber. A short time later, the airmen were rescued!

The pigeon was celebrated as a heroine on the RAF base, basking on her perch during a festive dinner held in her honour. The grateful airmen whose lives she saved decided she deserved to have a proper name—they called her Winkie, inspired by the story of her blinking eye.

Winkie was later awarded the first PDSA Dickin Medal for her bravery and devotion to duty.

DID YOU KNOW?
After Winkie died, her owner donated her stuffed body and her PDSA Dickin Medal to the McManus Art Gallery and Museum in Dundee, where she is still on display today.

Wojtek Soldier Bear

Wojtek was an orphaned bear that captured the heart of two countries and remains a symbol of the very special friendship between Scotland and Poland.

Wojtek's story began in 1942, when Polish soldiers heading to fight with the Allied Forces adopted an orphaned bear cub. They named him Wojtek, which means "Joyful Warrior" in Polish, and made him the mascot for the Polish Army's 22nd Transport Company. The bear made them laugh and gave them hope after all the terrible things they'd been through.

Animals were not allowed in the army so Wojtek was enlisted as a soldier, with his own paybook, rank and serial number. He was also given double rations of food!

By the time the Polish Army reached the war zone in Italy, Wojtek was fully grown and could march and salute just like the other soldiers.

During the Battle of Monte Cassino in 1944, Wojtek helped carry heavy crates of ammunition from the supply trucks to soldiers fighting on the front lines. He did this under heavy gunfire all night long, back and forth, never dropping a single box.

After the battle was won, the official emblem created for the 22nd Transport Company was an image of Wojtek carrying a shell. All the soldiers wore it with great pride on their uniforms.

Many Polish soldiers went to live in Scotland after the war, including Wojtek. He settled in to his new home at the Edinburgh Zoo and quickly became a star attraction.

The BBC children's programme Blue Peter came out to film him and his photos frequently appeared in magazines.

When Wojtek passed away at age 22, news of his death was reported around the world.

LIFE AT THE ZOO

Wotjek enjoyed people watching and was fascinated by the zoo's daily penguin parade.

He always turned his head if he heard someone speak Polish and was delighted whenever his old army buddies visited him. They often jumped across the ditch to wrestle with him!

WOJTEK'S MEMORIAL

A bronze statue in Edinburgh's Princes Street Gardens honours Wojtek and the Polish soldiers who fought so bravely for the Allies.

The statue shows the much-loved bear and a Polish Army soldier walking side by side.

Wopsie Trans-Atlantic Adventurer

A century ago, a tabby kitten named Wospie was the mascot aboard the first airship that travelled across the Atlantic—twice! The journey from Scotland to America and back again was one of the greatest feats of aviation.

Joining Wopsie on the flight was a young stowaway named William Ballantyne. He didn't want to miss out on the adventure of a lifetime, so when no one was looking he hid in the cramped space between the girders.

He was found 12 hours after the launch, when he became ill from the fumes leaking from the gas bags. As soon as he recovered, he was put to work as a cook for the crew.

Wopsie spent a good deal of time with William in the galley of the airship. For such a wee kitten, she had a HUGE appetite.

The Captain made a note in the ship's log that mentions her purring in one crew member's lap, always keeping a watchful eye on the food.

Finding a stowaway onboard wasn't the only drama Wopsie experienced on her history-making journey. The airship was caught up in a terrible storm and there was nothing to be done but ride it out. Poor Wopsie! Things finally calmed down and land was sighted far in the distance.

The R34 touched down on Long Island, New York, greeted by thousands of spectators and U.S. President Woodrow Wilson. Wopsie's photo appeared in newspapers and everyone wanted to meet her.

One wealthy American lady even offered to buy the furry adventurer for $1,000. That was a lot of money back then (and still is today).

The airship's engineer refused to sell her. He didn't want the first cat to cross the Atlantic to end up in a foreign land. Wopsie was a Scottish cat and belonged back in Scotland!

Not for sale

WOPSIE, THE MUSICAL

The year 2019 marks the 100th anniversary of the historic R34 flight.

Various celebrations are planned, including a musical entitled 'All Aboard the R34!'

The show features not just one but two songs about the airship's high-flying feline mascot.

Timeline

1818 – Torty is born, a year before Queen Victoria

1919 – Wopsie crosses the Atlantic in an airship

1940 – Bamse becames Norwegian Navy mascot

1941 – Gordon Highlanders in Singapore adopt Peggy

1942 – Winkie saves bomber crew in the North Sea

1944 – Wojtek helps Polish soldiers win WWII battle

1944 – Donald's eggs save starving POWs in the Far East

1944 – Sheila finds American aircrew lost in a blizzard

1944 – Princess Elizabeth receives Susan as a gift

1980 – Hercules goes missing in the Outer Hebrides

1970s/80s – Towser reigns as Glenturret's Chief Mouser

1987 – Artist creates ceramic 'replicats' of Smudge

1996 – Dolly's historic birth makes headlines

1996 – Hamish the Highland Bull's life is spared

2002 – Talavera marks her Drum Horse debut

2008 – Sir Nils Olav III receives a knighthood

2011 – Oswald becomes full-time museum moggy

2012 – Cruachan IV named Royal Regiment mascot

2012 – PD Sweep becomes UK's only poison detection dog

2013 – Baron models for *The Kelpies* sculptures

2013 – Socks becomes an internet sensation

2015 – Parsley goes on his first Oban walkabout

2016 – Golden George appointed first Ambassadog

2017 – William meets the Canadian Prime Minister

2018 – Kylie stuns scientists by "speaking" porpoise

More for Curious Minds

PLACES

Balmoral Castle, Ballater
balmoralcastle.com

Drum Castle, Drumoak
nts.org.uk

Edinburgh Zoo, Edinburgh
edinburghzoo.org.uk

Clyde Porpoise, North Ayrshire
clydeporpoise.org

Glenturret Distillery, Crieff
theglenturret.com

The Gordon Highlanders Museum, Aberdeen
gordonhighlanders.org.uk

Highland Wildlife Park, Kincraig
highlandwildlifepark.org.uk

Loch Ness
lochness.com

McManus Art Gallery & Museum, Dundee
mcmanus.co.uk

National Museum of Scotland, Edinburgh
nms.ac.uk

Oban
oban.org.uk

Rosslyn Chapel, Roslin
rosslynchapel.com

RSS Discovery, Dundee
rssdiscovery.com

Shetland Islands
shetland.org

The Stirling Smith Art Gallery and Museum, Stirling
smithartgalleryandmuseum.co.uk

St Andrews, Fife
visitstandrews.com

BOOKS

All the Queen's Corgis by Penny Junor

Hamish McHamish: Legend of St Andrews by Susan McMullan

Hamish: His Story by Angela and Craig Mair

Hercules the Bear: A Gentle Giant in the Family by Maggie Robin

Seadog Bamse: WWII Canine Hero by Andrew Orr

Rebel Cats: Brave Tales of Feisty Felines by Kimberlie Hamilton

William the Cat & the Rescue of Rosslyn Chapel by the Countess of Rosslyn

Wojtek the Soldier Bear by Ailene Orr

About the Author

Kimberlie Hamilton has written all sorts of things over the years, but what she loves most of all is writing entertaining nonfiction books for young and curious minds.

She believes that everyone and everything has a fascinating story to tell, if one simply knows how to observe and which questions to ask.

Kimberlie has two Master's degrees, one in screenwriting from the University of California and another in Cultural & Creative Communication from the University of Aberdeen.

She has a passion for exploring, learning, and helping animals in need, and lives in Scotland with her four cats, Scout, Sammy Jo, Whiskers and Elsa.

kimberliehamilton.co.uk

SCOTLAND'S

Animal Superstars

True Stories About Braw Birds & Beasties

by Kimberlie Hamilton

A portion of the royalties from this book will be donated to the Scottish SPCA

Shout Outs

BAMSE – Dr Andrew Orr, Montrose Heritage Trust

BARON – Andy Scott and Lorraine Clark

CRUACHAN IV – Pvt. Robert Buchanan, Karen Buchanan and Pony Major Mark Wilkinson, all of the Royal Regiment of Scotland

DONALD – Stewart Mitchell and Ruth Duncan, The Gordon Highlanders Museum

GOLDEN GEORGE – Erin Hickey, VisitScotland; Victoria and Emma Rae

HAMISH – Myra Kyle, Trossachs Woollen Mill

KYLIE – Friends of the Firth of Clyde; David Nairn, Clyde Porpoise Marine Mammal Project

OSWALD – Dr Elsbeth King; Michael McGinnes, Stirling Smith Art Gallery & Museum

PARSLEY – Fiona Ferris and Tam Ferris

PD SWEEP – Rhona Meikle

PEGGY – Stewart Mitchell and Ruth Duncan, The Gordon Highlanders Museum

SHEILA – Amy Dickin, PDSA

SIR NILS OLAV – Kayleigh Ross and Harriet Good, Edinburgh Zoo

SMUDGE – Dr Elsbeth King

SOCKS – Mari Williamson

TALAVERA – Jeanette Allen, Steven Grice and Alice Morgan of The Horse Trust

TORTY – Aidan McAleese, National Trust for Scotland, Drum Castle

TOWSER – Tracey MacIntosh and Gemma McColl, Glenturret Distillery

WILLIAM – Ian Gardner, Rosslyn Chapel

WINKIE – Dr Guy Puzey, Edinburgh University; Carly Cooper, McManus Galleries

WOJTEK – Harriet Good and Kayleigh Ross, Edinburgh Zoo

WOPSIE – Alastair Dodds, National Museums Scotland; Richard Wiles, Aerostat; Basil Abbott, Diss Museum

MISC – Glen Moyer, Under the Tartan Sky; Laura Moore, Scottish SCPA; Wendy Turner, Airedale Terrier Club of Scotland; John Otto; and the California Cats.

Photo Credits

We would like to thank the following for permission to reproduce various photos and images.

COVER
St Bernard/ ESIGHT, Tortoiseshell Persian Kitten/ kovalvs, Giant Tortoise/ Smileus, White Duck/ bazilfoto, Sitting Brown Bear/ JackF, Pigeon/ khunaspix, Sheep Isolated/ Innastakhova, Emperor Penguin / kotomiti all © Can Stock Photo

INTRO & END
Nessie Replica/ Stara Blazkova, Czech Wikipedia [CC BY-SA 3.0]
Wild Haggis/ Stara Blazkova) [CC BY-SA 4.0]
Pets/ Scottish SPCA

BAMSE
Bamse in Sailor Cap, Ship, and Statue Unveiling/ all © Montrose Heritage Trust
Painted rock on grave/ ©Kimberlie Hamilton Bamse Painting/ © Felicity Ivory / Montrose Heritage Trust

BARON
Wedding, Two Horses, Horse Show, Baron & Kelpie Duo Profile/ all © Lorraine Clark

CRUCHAN IV
Pony Major and New Stripes, Welcoming Queen/ all Mark Owens, © MOD Crown Copyright
The Duke & Duchess of Sussex Mark Jones [CC BY 2.0]

DOLLY
Dolly Parton/ Eva Rinaldi [CC BY-SA 2.0]
DNA Illustration/ rob3000, Scientist in Lab/ gajdamak, Scottish Fold Kitten/ LeniKovaleva, Two Little Lambs/ ESIGHT, Sheep Isolated/ Innastakhova all © Can Stock Photo
Dolly the Sheep/ Toni Barros [CC BY-SA 2.0]

DONALD
Arriving in Aberdeen, Introducing Ducklings to Water, and William Gray/ all © The Gordon Highlanders Museum

GOLDEN GEORGE
Official Castle, Red Bandana all © VisitScotland/Duke Photography
Red Carpet/ © Eoin Carey/Glasgow Film Festival
Greyfriars Bobby/ Michael Reeve [CC BY-SA 3.0]

HAMISH
Hamish at the Museum © The Stirling Smith Art Gallery and Museum
"Cattle" Painting by Joseph Denovan Adam © The Stirling Smith Art Gallery and Museum

HERCULES
Hercules the Bear/ Ivanbalich [CC BY-SA 3.0] Hercules Birthday Cake/ Trinity Mirror / Mirrorpix / Alamy Stock

KYLIE
Kylie Leaping/ © David Nairn, Clyde Porpoise Project & Common Dolphin NOAA NMFS [Public Domain]

OSWALD
CU of Oswald/ © John Otto
Oswald Next to Painting/ The Stirling Smith Art Gallery and Museum (painting by Silvia Anestikova) and With Catnip and Old Football/ The Stirling Smith Art Gallery and Museum
Stirling Castle/ phbcz © Can Stock Photo

PARSLEY
All Parsley photos/ © Fiona Ferris

PD SWEEP
Sweep and Rhona Meikle/ © PDSA, All other photos/ © Rhona Meikle

PEGGY
Grainy full length shot and Major Reggie Lees/ © The Gordon Highlanders Museum
Gravestone/ © Kimberlie Hamilton

SHEILA
Sheila with John Dagg/ © PDSA, Sheila with Maria Dickin/ © PDSA

The Scottish SPCA

The **Scottish Society for the Prevention of Cruelty to Animals** (Scottish SPCA) is Scotland's animal welfare charity.

Their inspectors save thousands of domestic, farm and wild animals from harm and danger every year, while their rescue and rehoming centre vets and staff look after, rehabilitate, release and find new homes for thousands more.

A portion of the royalties from *Scotland's Animal Superstars* will be donated to the Scottish SPCA to help make this country a kinder and better place for all animals.

For more information visit:

www.scottishspca.org